AF605676
N
W
E
S
QLD
QUEENSLAND
SA
SOUTH
AUSTRALIA
NSW
NEW SOUTH WALES
ACT
AUSTRALIAN
CAPITAL
TERRITORY
VIC
VICTORIA
TAS
TASMANIA

KYLE SURRY
KIDS' GUIDE TO AUSTRALIA'S STATES & TERRITORIES
DISCOVERING
TAS
TASMANIA
REDBACK
publishing

First Published 2026 by
Redback Publishing
Suite 6, 13a Narabang Way,
Belrose NSW 2085
Australia

www.redbackpublishing.com
orders@redbackpublishing.com

ISBN 978-1-761400-65-0

Author: Kyle Surry
Editors: Lucinda Dodds and Emma Dobinson
Designer: Redback Publishing

MIX
Paper from responsible sources
FSC www.fsc.org FSC™ C001507

Original illustrations © Redback Publishing 2026
Originated by Redback Publishing

Acknowledgements
Abbreviations: l—left, r—right, b—bottom, t—top, c—centre, m—middle
We would like to thank the following for permission to reproduce photographs: (Images © shutterstock, Alamy) p4-5 - Robert Hawker Dowling - Robert Dowling | Group of Natives of Tasmania, Public Domain, https://commons.wikimedia.org/w/index.php?curid=12635841, p6-7 - Francois Geoffroi Roux - Scanned from L'Empire des Mers, Martine Acerra & Jean MeyerMarines editorISBN 2826401009, Public Domain, https://commons.wikimedia.org/w/index.php?curid=3134077, p7br - John Glover - http://acms.sl.nsw.gov.au/item/itemDetailPaged.aspx?itemID=404681, Public Domain, https://commons.wikimedia.org/w/index.php?curid=26606315, p10-11 - Rachael Bowes / Shutterstock.com, p14-15 - Alistair McLellan / Shutterstock.com, p17mr - Steve Lovegrove / Shutterstock.com, p20br - Claudine Van Massenhove / Shutterstock.com, p21bl - TK Kurikawa / Shutterstock.com, p22-23 - Ikonya / Shutterstock.com, p25tl - Squiresy92 including elements from Sodacan - Own work, CC BY-SA 4.0, https://commons.wikimedia.org/w/index.php?curid=47817451, p26-27 - AlecTrusler2015 / Shutterstock.com, p27mr- haireena / Shutterstock.com

NATIONAL LIBRARY OF AUSTRALIA
A catalogue record for this book is available from the National Library of Australia

CONTENTS

A Long Time Ago	4
Colony of Tasmania	6
Where Is Tasmania?	8
How Many People?	10
The Biggest Cities	12
Getting Around in Tasmania	14
Farms and Food	16
Wilderness	18
Special Places in Tasmania	20
Government of Tasmania	22
Flags of Tasmania	24
Emblems of Tasmania	25
Antarctica	26
Tasmanian Tiger	28
Tasmanian Devil	30
Glossary	31
Index	32

Port Arthur Lavender Farm

A LONG TIME AGO

Who Was There First?

Over 40,000 years ago, ancestors of Indigenous Australians walked into Tasmania when it was joined to the rest of Australia by dry land.

Some of the Indigenous nations of Tasmania:

- Lairmairrener
- Nuenonne
- Paredarerme
- Peerapper
- Tommeginne
- Toogee

Tasmanian Indigenous women were making beautiful shell necklaces thousands of years ago.

Maireener (also known as Rainbow Kelp) shells, which were used in traditional shell necklace-making.

The Black War in the 1820s was a time of many battles between the Indigenous people of Tasmania and the settlers from Britain.

Kutikina Cave

The rock art and tools found in the Kutikina Cave show that Indigenous Australians were living there up to 30,000 years ago.

COLONY OF TASMANIA

Abel Tasman, a Dutch explorer, sailed to Tasmania in 1642. He named it Van Diemen's Land. No-one was sure if Tasmania was an island or not until Bass and Flinders sailed all around it in 1798. Van Diemen's Land was part of the British colony of New South Wales until 1825. In 1856, the name was changed to Tasmania.

1804

Convicts from Britain began to build the first settlements at Hobart and Launceston.

1800s

Migration posters used in Europe said that Tasmania had no droughts and the best climate in the world!

WHERE IS TASMANIA?

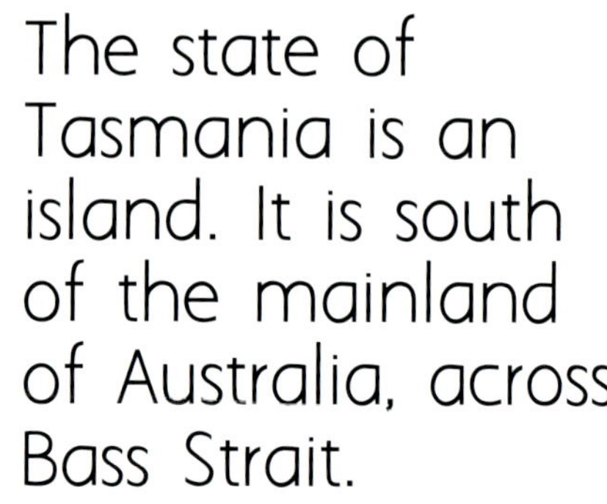

The state of Tasmania is an island. It is south of the mainland of Australia, across Bass Strait.

The capital city is Hobart. Tasmania's shortened name is written as TAS. Tasmania wasn't always an island. It was joined to Australia by land until the oceans rose about 12,000 years ago.

Where are the borders of Tasmania?

Northern border:
Bass Strait

Eastern border:
Tasman Sea

Western border:
Great Australian Bight

Tasmania

Southern border:
Southern Ocean

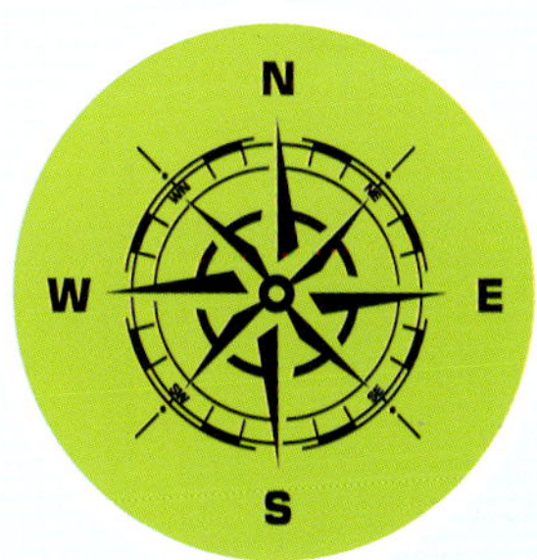

South East Cape is the most southerly point of Australia. Keep going south from there and you will reach Antarctica.

HOW MANY PEOPLE?

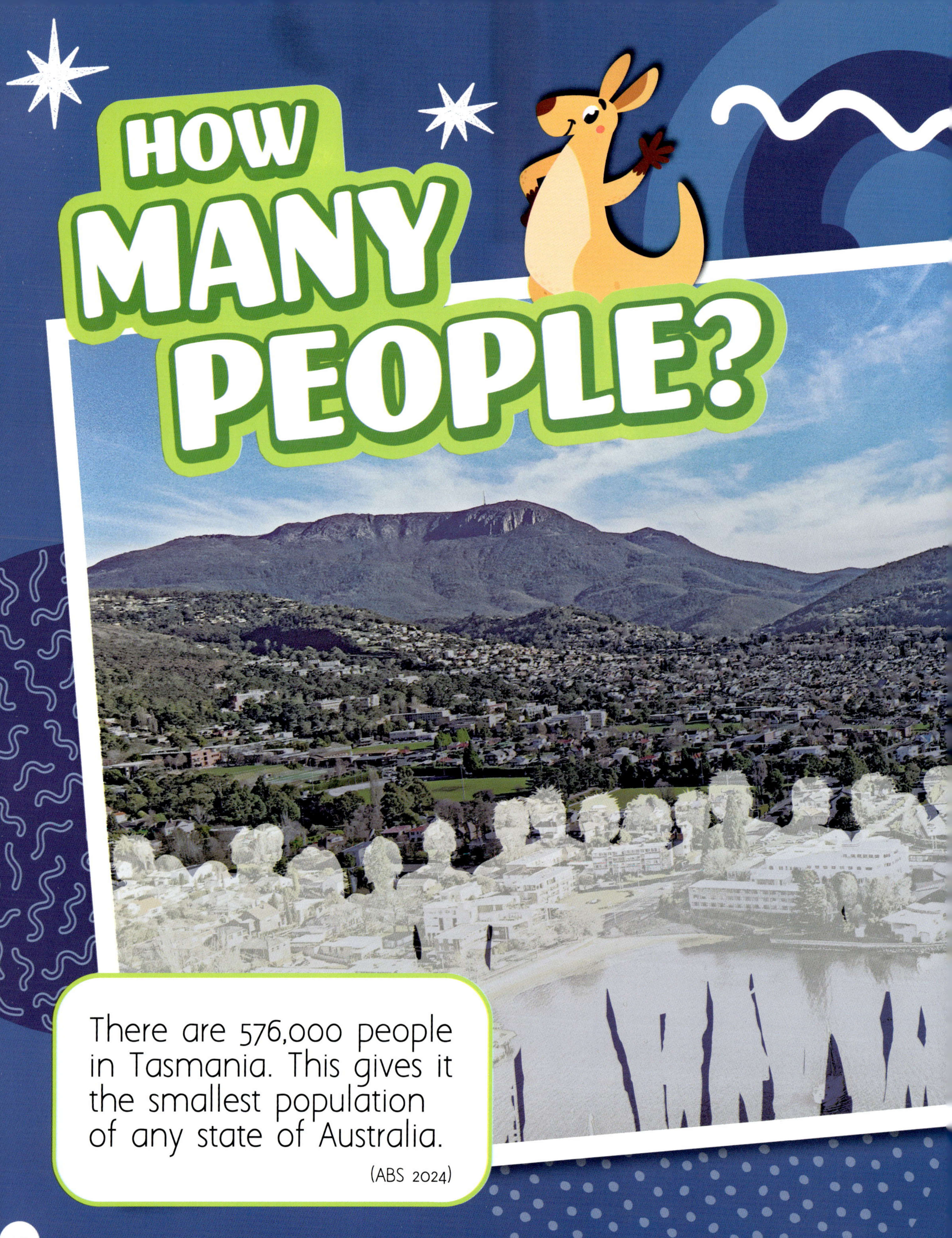

There are 576,000 people in Tasmania. This gives it the smallest population of any state of Australia.

(ABS 2024)

Two out of every three people in Tasmania do not live in the capital city area near Hobart. In the other states of Australia, most people live near their capital city.

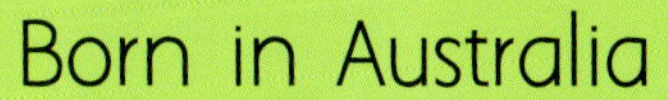

In 2021, about 15% of people in Tasmania were born overseas. The top countries of birth outside Australia were England, China, Nepal and India.

(ABS 2022)

There are about nine times more people just in Sydney and its suburbs than there are in all of the state of Tasmania.

THE BIGGEST CITIES

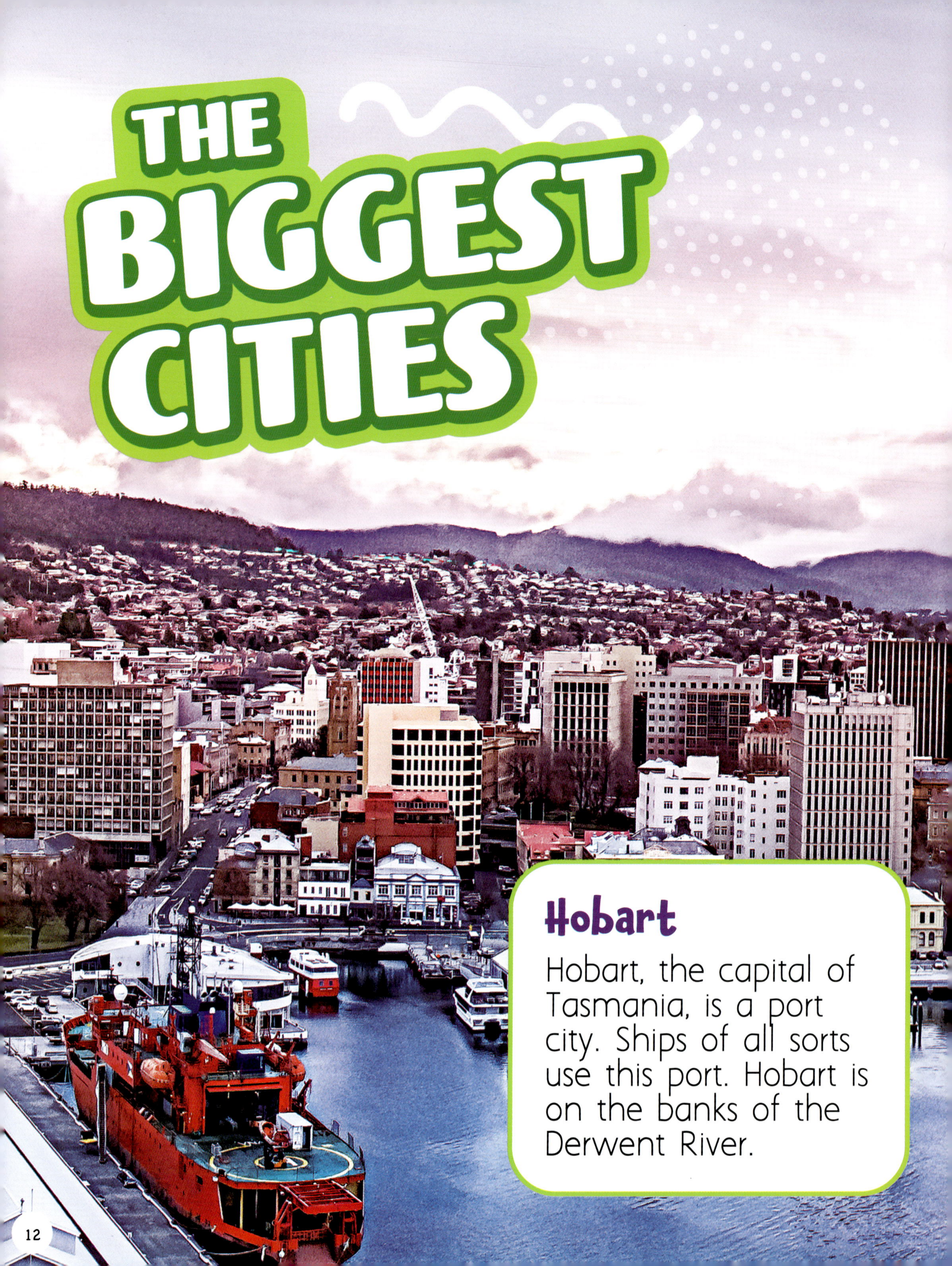

Hobart

Hobart, the capital of Tasmania, is a port city. Ships of all sorts use this port. Hobart is on the banks of the Derwent River.

Launceston

Launceston, the second largest city in Tasmania, is on the Tamar River. It is in the north of Tasmania.

Devonport

This is the third biggest city in Tasmania. It is in the north of the state, on the banks of the Mersey River.

Burnie

Burnie is on the north coast of Tasmania. It has one of the busiest cargo shipping ports in Australia.

GETTING AROUND IN TASMANIA

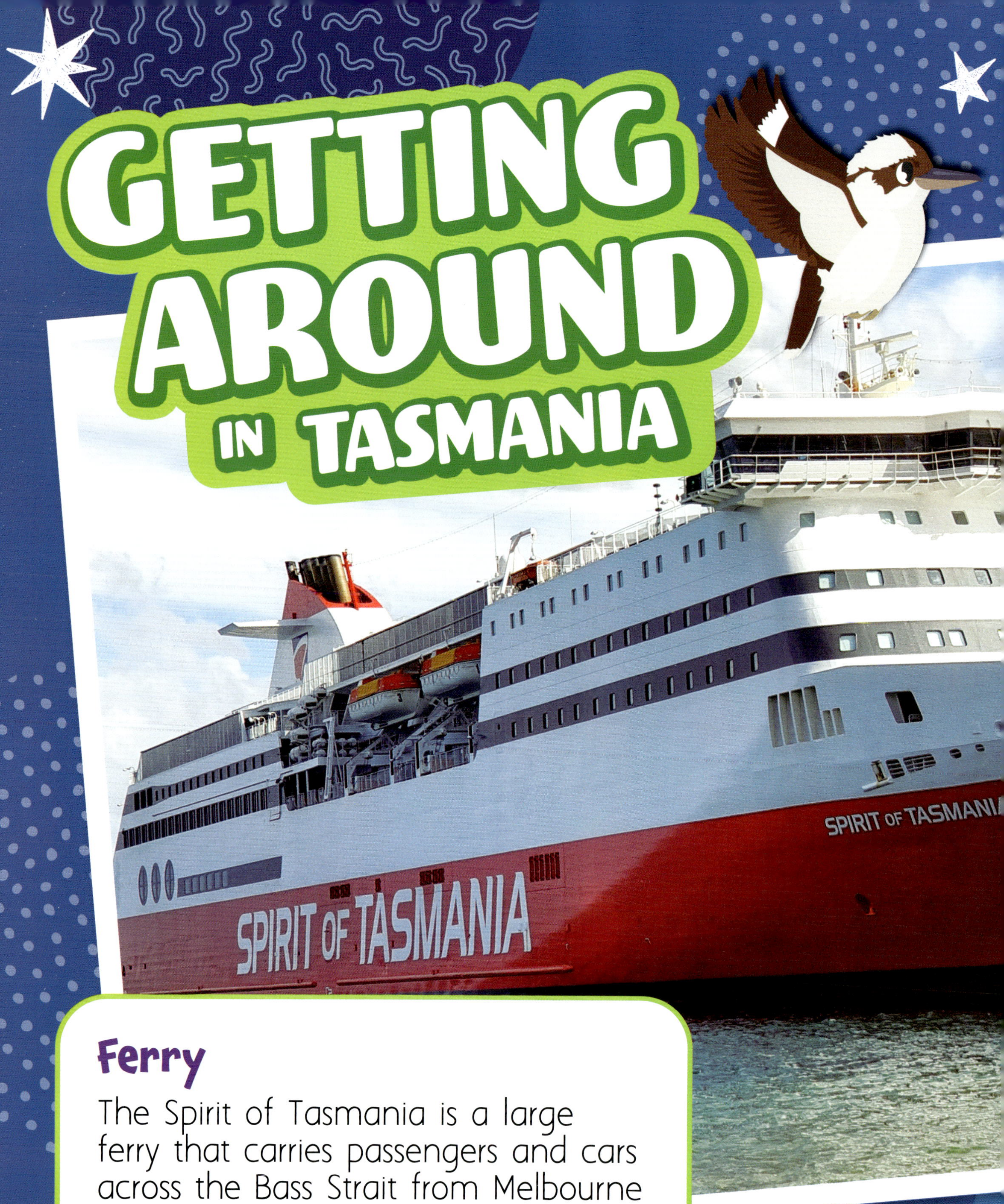

Ferry

The Spirit of Tasmania is a large ferry that carries passengers and cars across the Bass Strait from Melbourne in Victoria to Devonport in Tasmania.

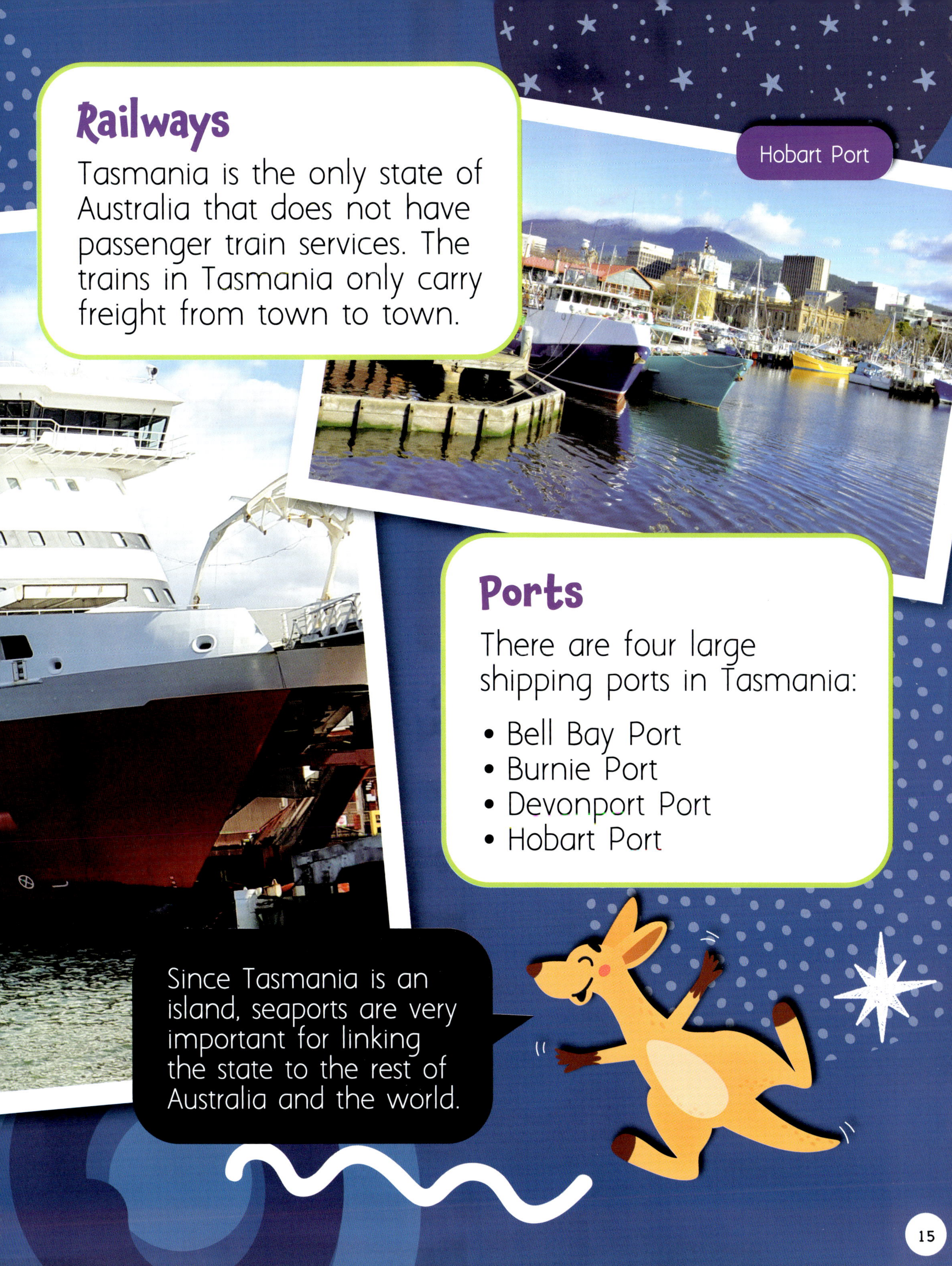

Railways

Tasmania is the only state of Australia that does not have passenger train services. The trains in Tasmania only carry freight from town to town.

Ports

There are four large shipping ports in Tasmania:

- Bell Bay Port
- Burnie Port
- Devonport Port
- Hobart Port

Since Tasmania is an island, seaports are very important for linking the state to the rest of Australia and the world.

One quarter of the land in Tasmania is used for farming. The produce is exported to the rest of Australia and overseas.

Lavender

Products include the oils from lavender, peppermint and many other plants.

Milk and Cheese

Tasmania's climate is good for producing high quality dairy products. The dairies on King Island are well-known for their cheeses.

Salmon

Salmon fishing and farming is one of Tasmania's biggest industries.

Clean and Green

Tasmania's air has been tested and it is some of the best anywhere! The clean air and water in Tasmania make it a great place for farming.

Drugs

Some Tasmanian farmers can legally grow opium poppies. These are turned into drugs used in medicine. A large proportion of the world's legal opium poppies are grown in Tasmania.

WILDERNESS

The Tasmanian Wilderness World Heritage Area covers about a quarter of the whole state.

The Cradle Mountain-Lake St Clair National Park is one of the few temperate wilderness areas left in the Southern Hemisphere. The area includes Lake Pedder, which was created in 1972 when a dam was built so that its water could be used to generate electricity.

Gordon Dam at Lake Pedder

Lake St Clair is the deepest lake in Australia and the source of the Derwent River.

In 1983, the Franklin River was saved from having a dam built across it. It is now a beautiful wilderness area.

SPECIAL PLACES IN TASMANIA

Biggest Islands

- Flinders Island
- King Island
- Macquarie Island

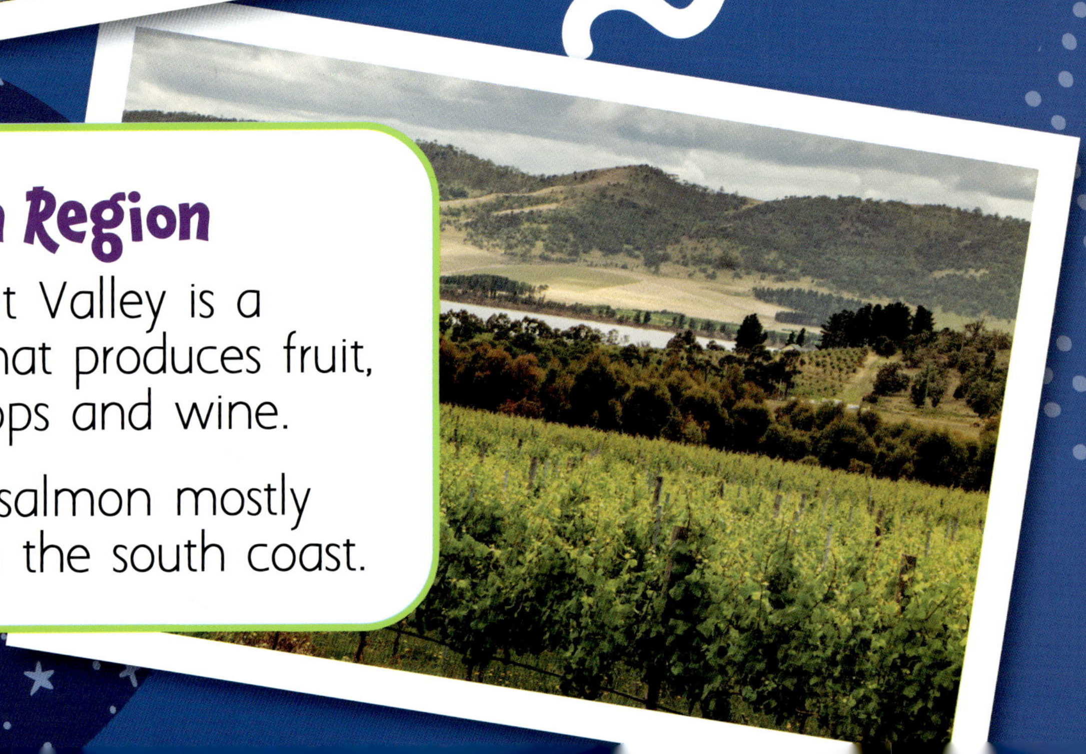

Southern Region

The Derwent Valley is a rural area that produces fruit, potatoes, hops and wine.

Tasmanian salmon mostly comes from the south coast.

Highlands

The highlands are in the central part of Tasmania, where there are both mountains and pastures.

Port Arthur

From 1830 to 1877, Port Arthur was a jail for convicts.

Salamanca Markets

These outdoor markets have been one of Tasmania's favourite tourist spots since 1972.

GOVERNMENT OF TASMANIA

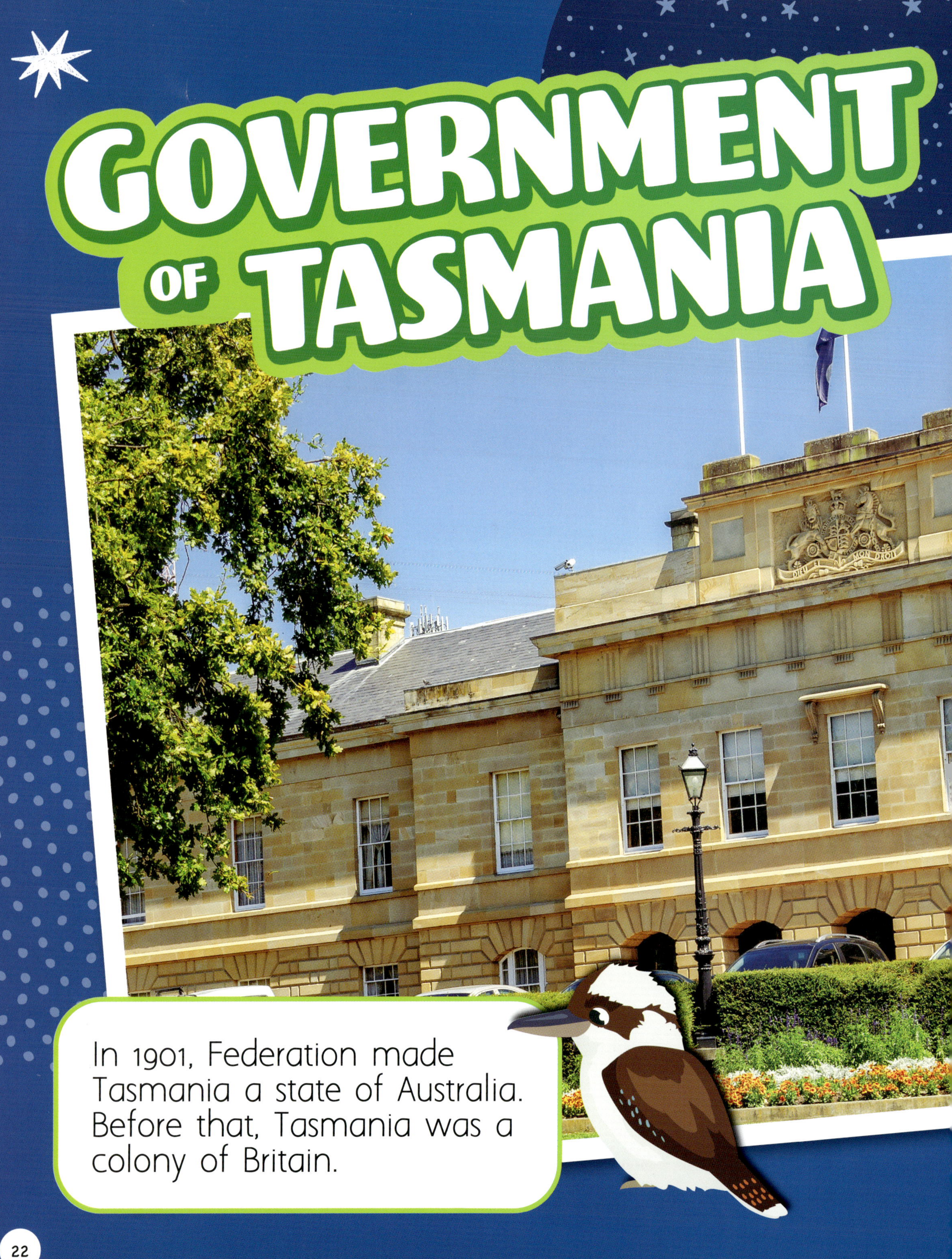

In 1901, Federation made Tasmania a state of Australia. Before that, Tasmania was a colony of Britain.

Tasmanian State Parliament

The Legislative Council (Upper House) has 15 members.

The House of Assembly (Lower House) has 35 members.

Australian Senate

Tasmania also has 12 Senators in the Australian Parliament in Canberra. This means it has as many Senators as the bigger states, even though its population is so small.

There are only five Federal electorates in Tasmania: Bass, Braddon, Denison, Franklin, Lyons.

Tasmania's five Federal electorates

FLAGS OF TASMANIA

Australian Aboriginal Flag

The Aboriginal Flag was first flown in 1971. It was designed by elder Harold Thomas in 1970.

What the flag represents:

Yellow Disc	The Sun and yellow ochre
Red	The land
Black	The Aboriginal people of Australia

Tasmanian State Flag

The Tasmanian state flag was only made official in 1975, but it had been used since 1875.

EMBLEMS OF TASMANIA

Floral Emblem
Tasmanian flowering blue gum

Animal Emblem
Tasmanian devil

Mineral Emblem
Crocoite

The Coat of Arms

This is a symbol of Tasmania and each part of it has a meaning.

Animals
Two Tasmanian tigers support a shield topped by a lion

Motto
The Latin motto *Ubertas et Fidelitas* means 'Fruitfulness and Faithfulness'

Farming
Wheat, apples, hops and sheep represent agriculture

Mining
The red lion holding a pick and shovel represents mining

ANTARCTICA

Hobart is one of the few cities in the world where ships and aircraft leaving for Antarctica can stock up with the supplies they will need.

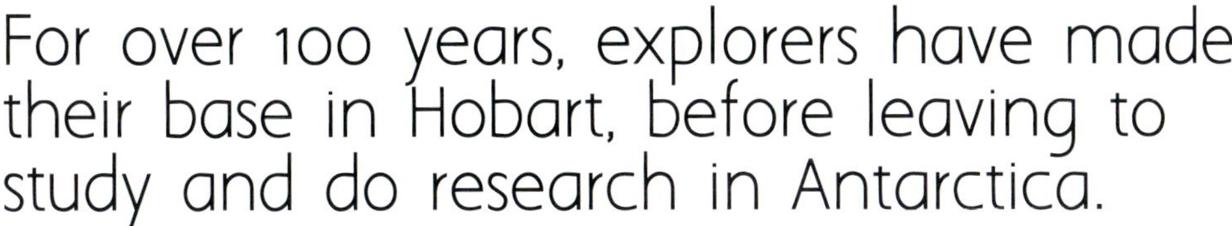

For over 100 years, explorers have made their base in Hobart, before leaving to study and do research in Antarctica.

In 1911, Roald Amundsen left from Hobart to lead the first team to reach the South Pole.

Between 1911 and 1914, Australian explorer, Douglas Mawson, also studied Antarctica after leaving from Hobart.

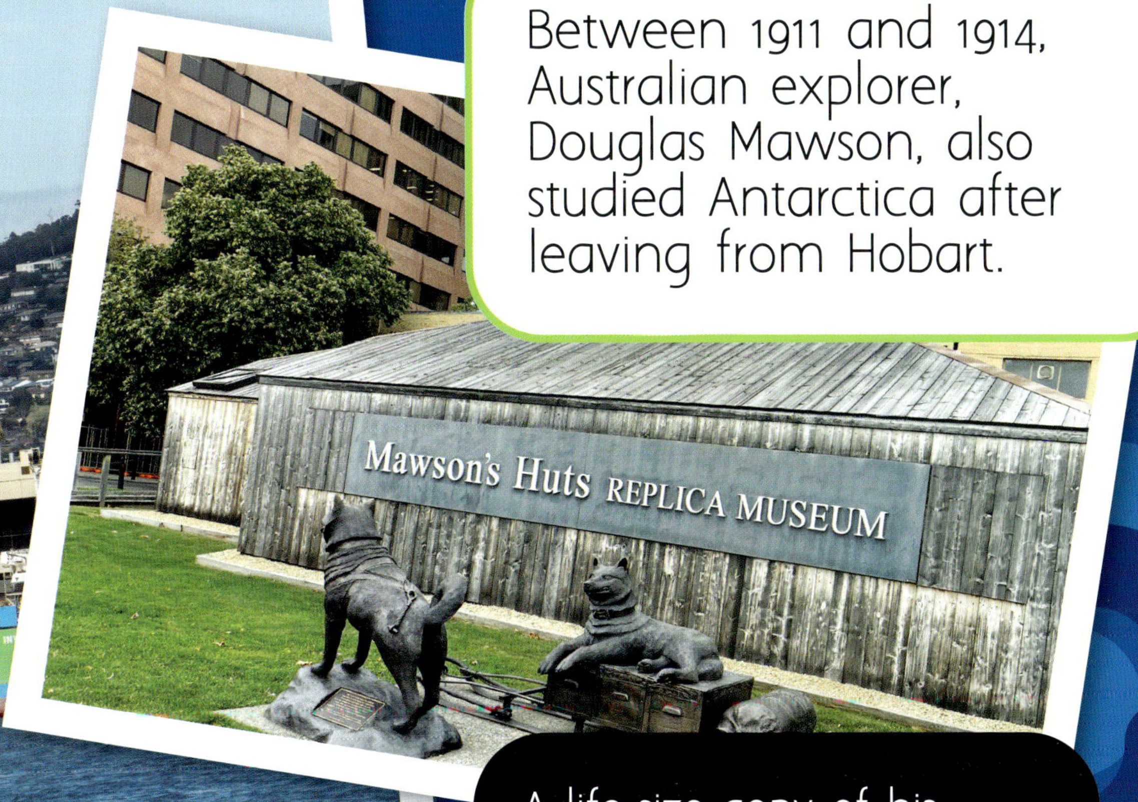

A life-size copy of his Antarctic hut is in Hobart.

TASMANIAN TIGER

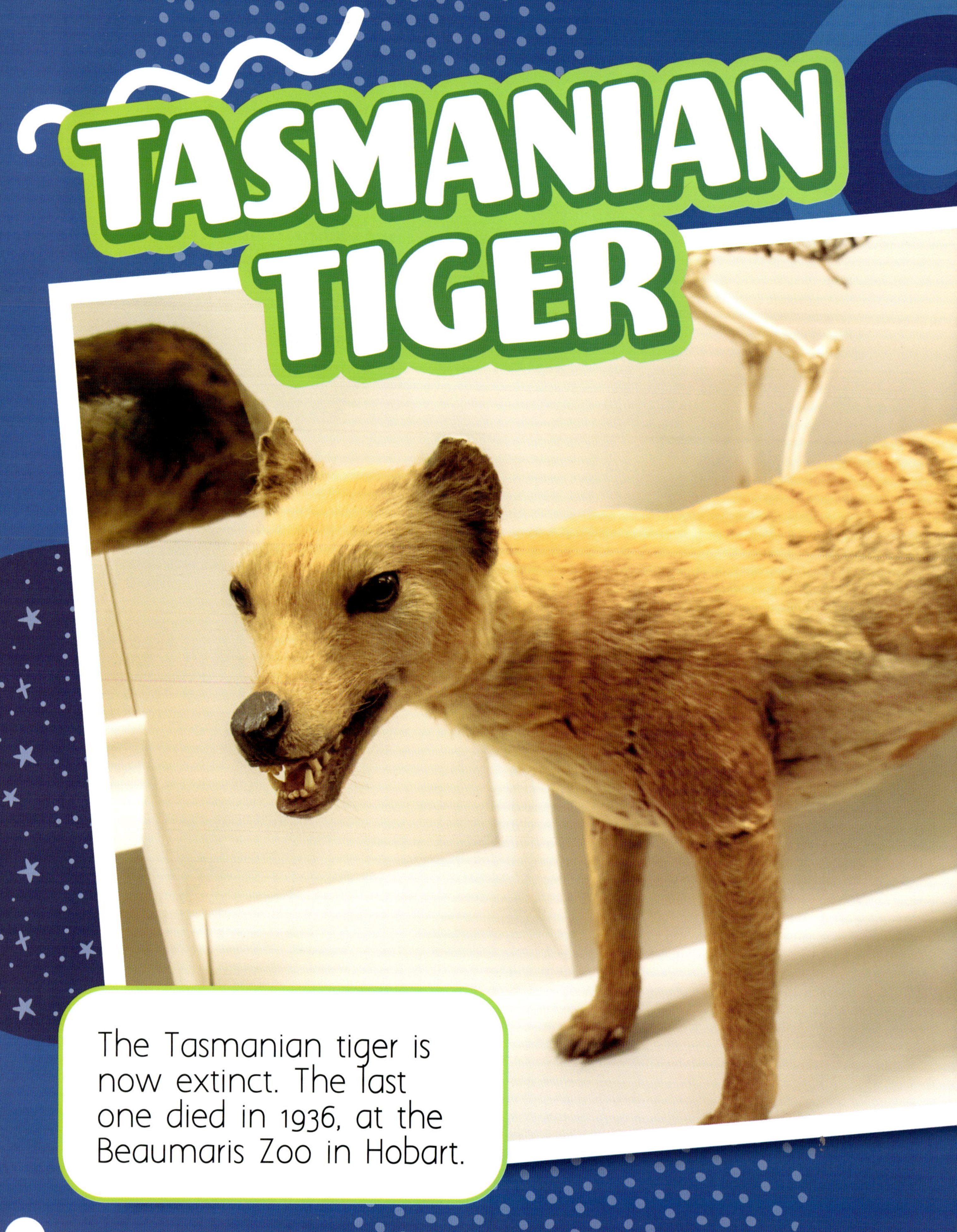

The Tasmanian tiger is now extinct. The last one died in 1936, at the Beaumaris Zoo in Hobart.

The Tasmanian tiger was a marsupial tiger, and a very rare and special animal.
Some people think that there might still be some left alive, hiding in the forests of Tasmania.

TASMANIAN DEVIL

Tasmanian devils make a loud, screeching noise and they often fight with each other. They have a very strong bite!

The little Tasmanian devil is a marsupial that was close to becoming extinct. A plan was put into action to save them, and their numbers have now increased.

The Tasmanian devil is not safe yet. They suffer from a cancer that affects their faces. They are also still killed by feral dogs.

cargo freight

colonists people who move to a new country and impose their culture on it

dairy place where cows are milked and milk products made

emblem symbol

extinct none left alive

freight goods that are carried from place to place, usually for sale

fruitfulness producing lots of offspring

hops plant used to make beer

opium drug

represent stand in place of

settlers people who move to live in a different country, usually as farmers

Southern Hemisphere lower half of planet Earth

strait narrow sea between two pieces of land

Cradle Mountain National Park

INDEX

Bass Strait 8, 9, 14
Black War 5
Burnie 13
Derwent River 12, 19, 20
Devonport 13, 14
ferry 14
Hobart 7, 8, 11, 12, 26-28
Kutikina Cave 5
Lake St Clair 18, 19
Launceston 7, 13
South East Cape 9

Burnie

Tasmanian Salmon

KIDS' GUIDE
TO
AUSTRALIA'S
STATES & TERRITORIES
WA
WESTERN
AUSTRALIA
NT
NORTHERN
TERRITORY